**CELEBRATE
HOLIDAYS**

Celebrate
Christmas

Joanne Mattern

The nutcracker is one of many Christmas symbols.

 Enslow Publishers, Inc.
40 Industrial Road
Box 398
Berkeley Heights, NJ 07922
USA

http://www.enslow.com

Library of Congress Cataloging-in-Publication Data

Mattern, Joanne, 1963–
   Celebrate Christmas / Joanne Mattern.
     p. cm. — (Celebrate holidays)
   Includes bibliographical references and index.
   ISBN-13: 978-0-7660-2776-3
   ISBN-10: 0-7660-2776-7
     1. Christmas—Juvenile literature. I. Title.
   GT4985.M374 2007
   394.2663—dc22

                        2006025258

Printed in the United States of America

10 9 8 7 6 5 4 3 2 1

To Our Readers: We have done our best to make sure all Internet Addresses in this book were active and appropriate when we went to press. However, the author and the publisher have no control over and assume no liability for the material available on those Internet sites or on other Web sites they may link to. Any comments or suggestions can be sent by e-mail to comments@ enslow.com or to the address on the back cover.

Every effort has been made to locate all copyright holders of material used in this book. If any errors or omissions have occurred, corrections will be made in future editions of this book.

Illustration Credits: 10four Design, iStockphoto.com, p. 1; Art Media, Heritage-Images, The Image Works, p. 8; Associated Press, pp. 34, 40, 45, 46, 95; Associated Press, Pressens Bild, p. 55; Big Box of Art 615,000, pp. 2–3, 4–5 (background), 12–13 (background), 35 (background), 46–47 (background), 61 (background), 87 (background), 98–99 (background); Corel Corporation, pp. 7, 68, 73, 80; Bob Daemmrich, The Image Works, pp. 53, 91; Fine Art Photographic Library, London / Art Resources, NY, p. 58; Hemera Photo Objects, pp. 5, 13, 35, 47, 61, 87; ©2006 Jupiterimages Corporation, pp. 4, 29, 50, 89, 96, 99; Library of Congress Prints and Photographs Division, pp. 49, 82; Mary Evans Picture Library, The Image Works, pp. 15, 26, 70; Masterfile/Masterfile, p. 86; Monika Graff, The Image Works, p. 78; North Wind/North Wind Picture Archives, p. 10; Picture Collection, The Branch Libraries, The New York Public Library, Astor, Lenox and Tilden Foundations, p. 42; PhotoEdit, Inc., p. 93; Réunion des Musées Nationaux, Art Resource, NY, p. 17; Shutterstock, pp. 12, 21, 32, 37, 57, 60, 63, 66, 69, 71, 72, 84.

Cover Illustration: 10four Design, iStockphoto.com.

CONTENTS

A Child Is Born

About two thousand years ago, a baby was born to a young couple in Bethlehem in the Middle East. But this was no ordinary birth. This child's birthday would become one of the most important and widely celebrated holidays in the world, and the baby would become one of the key religious figures in history. The baby's name was Jesus, and his birthday would eventually become the holiday known as Christmas.

A Biblical Birth

The story of Jesus' birth is told in two books of an important religious work called the Bible. These books are the gospel of Matthew and the gospel of Luke. Luke's gospel tells the story of an angel who visited a young girl named Mary. The angel told Mary that she would give birth to a child who is the son of God. A few months later, Mary and her new husband, Joseph, were forced to travel to Bethlehem from their home in Nazareth to be counted in a census. As Luke explains, "And while they were there, the time came for her to be delivered. And she gave birth to her first-born son and wrapped him in swaddling cloths, and laid him in a manger, because there was no place for them in the inn."[1]

Right away, it was clear that this was no ordinary birth. Luke goes on to say, "And in that region there were shepherds out in the field, keeping watch over their flock by night. And an angel of the Lord appeared to them, and the glory of the Lord shone around them, and they were filled with fear. And the angel said to them 'Be not afraid; for behold, I bring you good news of great joy which will come to all the people; for to you is born this day in the city of David a Savior, who is Christ the Lord.'"[2]

The birth of Jesus Christ is known as the Nativity, and people often use figurines to portray scenes like this in their homes and in their yards during Christmas time.

A 16th century painting of an angel alerting the shepherds of the birth of Jesus. At first, they are afraid of the divine messenger, but the angel assures them that he comes with good news—a Savior has been born.

A Historical Mystery

Years later, as Jesus became an important religious and historical figure, historians tried to pinpoint the exact circumstances of his birth. They used details from the Bible to try to identify historical events that would allow them to date Jesus' birth, or Nativity. One of the best clues is that Mary and Joseph traveled to Bethlehem to take part in a census during the rule of a Roman governor named Quirinius. This census is mentioned by an ancient historian named Flavius Josephus and occurred in the year 6 A.D.[3]

Another clue is the appearance of a bright star in the sky over the place where Jesus was born. The gospel of Matthew describes three kings, or wise men, who followed this star in search of the infant Jesus. Matthew wrote that the wise men said, "We have seen his star in the East, and have come to worship him."[4] The kings followed the star, which "went before them, till it came to rest over the place where the child was."[5] Historians think that this bright star might actually have been a lunar eclipse that occurred around 4 B.C.[6] This makes things even more complicated, since the two gospels do not even agree with each other on the year of Jesus' birth.

Some historians conclude that "Matthew and Luke chose two (or more) separate and contradictory oral traditions as the narrative of Jesus' birth. The fact that we cannot reconcile the two means that we cannot be sure when, or even where, Jesus was born, nor can we be sure of the events surrounding his birth."[7] The truth is, the historical details of Jesus' birth are impossible to prove. Things became even more confusing in the centuries that followed, as Christians took

A hand-colored woodcut of the star guiding the
three kings to baby Jesus. Some historians believe
that this mythical bright star, which led the three
wise men to Jesus, might have actually been a
lunar eclipse—when the moon is either partially
or completely hidden by the Earth's shadow.

pagan traditions and grafted religious beliefs onto them to create the holiday known as Christmas.

Christmas has a background unlike any other holiday. Is it a religious holiday? Is it a commercial holiday? Is it an American tradition or a worldwide celebration? The answer to these questions is "all of the above." Over the centuries, Christmas has become the most popular and well-known holiday. Its rich history makes it unique among celebrations and provides a treasure of images, ideas, and traditions.

A happy Christmas

The History of Christmas

Today, Christmas celebrates the birth of Jesus. However, winter celebrations had been held in December for centuries before Jesus' birth.

The Winter Solstice

Winter was a good time for feasting and celebration. The hard work of harvesting and hunting was done for the year, and planting did not need to be done until spring. Cattle were usually killed to provide fresh meat for the winter, and the meat had to be eaten before it spoiled. There was also plenty of beer and wine on hand. The combination of a light workload and plenty of food and drink meant it was a great time for a party.[1]

In the past, there were no electric lights or even lamps lit by gas or other fuel. The only artificial light was provided by candles, torches, or other forms of fire. Fire, while a powerful tool, did not provide much light compared to the sun. Ancient people knew that without the sun's light and warmth, they could not survive. Therefore, winter was a long and difficult season in the northern parts of the world.

Ancient people knew that the shortest day of the year fell around December 21. This day is called the winter solstice. Although three months of winter still lay ahead, people knew that the sun shone a little bit longer each day after December 21. For this reason, almost every ancient culture celebrated the shortest day of the year as the rebirth of the sun.[2] The ancient Vikings, who lived in the far northern lands of Scandinavia, celebrated the winter solstice by burning a huge log. They called this log the "yule log." The Vikings believed that the yule log would "drive away evil spirits, bring good luck to the people of the area,

These five children have found a very large log they are dragging home for burning, a tradition first celebrated by the Vikings who believed it brought them good luck.

and welcome the sun back to the skies."[3] People feasted and celebrated until the log burned out, which could take as long as twelve days.

Other ancient cultures also celebrated the rebirth of the sun. Early histories show that midwinter festivals were held in Babylon, Persia, and Egypt.

The Vikings

The Vikings are best known as pirates and brutal warriors. They lived in Scandinavia—the area that now makes up Denmark, Norway, and Sweden. The Vikings dominated European nations from the late 700s A.D. until 1100 A.D., so much so that European history remembers that time as the Viking Age. However, most Vikings were peaceful farmers.

Vikings advanced the art of shipbuilding so that their boats could sail to places never before reached. Vikings traveled across the North Atlantic to Iceland, Greenland, and even North America—roughly 500 years before Christopher Columbus. They briefly had a colony, which they called Vinland the Good, in what is now L'Anse aux Meadows, Newfoundland, Canada.

Saturnalia

Many ancient cultures worshiped more than one god. They believed that gods and goddesses ruled over different aspects of life and nature. The ancient Romans also had a midwinter celebration to honor a god. This celebration was called Saturnalia in honor of Saturn, the god of agriculture. Saturnalia began the week before the winter solstice and continued for a month. During

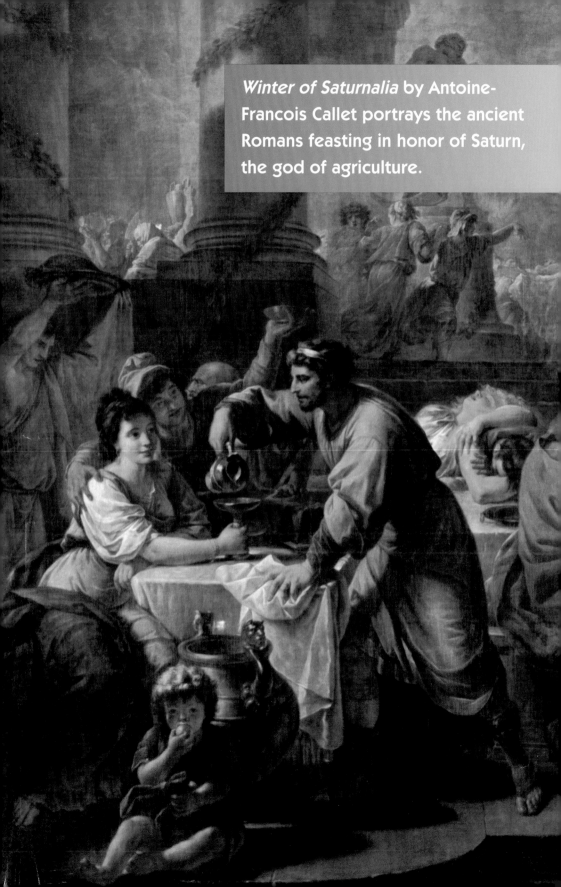

Winter of Saturnalia by Antoine-Francois Callet portrays the ancient Romans feasting in honor of Saturn, the god of agriculture.

this celebration, people feasted and drank. Businesses and schools closed. The social order was turned upside down. Slaves and masters switched places, and so did peasants and people of the upper classes. It was a wild time.[4] Part of the festivities included a celebration for the demi-god Mithras. Mithras was the son of a god and a human woman. He was called "the god of the unconquerable sun," and his birthday was celebrated on December 25.

Choosing December 25

During the first several centuries after the birth of Jesus, Christianity spread throughout Europe. Christmas celebrations, however, had no part in the early days of the church. Easter, which celebrates Jesus' resurrection from the dead, was the most important holiday in the church calendar.[5]

The first recorded celebration of Jesus' birth took place in 125 A.D., when Telesphorus, the second bishop of Rome, declared that church services that year should commemorate "the Nativity of our Lord and Savior."[6] Telesphorus did not suggest a specific birthdate for Jesus, so over the next two centuries, Jesus' birth was celebrated on more than a dozen different days. At the same time, many Christians continued to celebrate Saturnalia.

By 320, Pope Julius I had had enough of the different dates and celebrations of Jesus' birth. He announced that December 25 would be the feast day of Jesus' birth. Few people paid much attention to Pope Julius I's proclamation until 325. That year, Emperor Constantine the Great announced that Christmas would always be celebrated on December 25.[7] The word *Christmas* comes from combining the words "Christ's Mass."

At first glance, December 25 might seem like an odd choice to celebrate Jesus' birthday, because it is almost certain that he was not born in December. Although no date is recorded, biblical descriptions of the Nativity mention shepherds watching their flocks in the fields. Shepherds would not have their flocks out in the fields during December.

Pope Julius and Constantine had a specific reason for choosing December 25. They and other church leaders wanted to end pagan winter celebrations. They decided that because people were celebrating Saturnalia around December 25, that feast could simply be replaced by Christmas.[8]

Wild Celebrations

Gradually, the practice of celebrating Christmas spread throughout Europe and Asia. By the end of the eighth century, Christmas had spread all the way to Scandinavia.[9] It was an established Christian holiday. For a while, Christmas was a solemn feast day that people celebrated by going to Mass. By the Middle Ages, things had changed. Once again, Christmas became a time for parties and feasting.

On Christmas Day, people went to Mass at midnight or early in the morning. After they acknowledged Jesus' birth, they returned home to celebrate in a very different way than the solemn church services. Communities gathered for parties that included feasting and a great deal of drinking.

Christmas also became a time when the social order was turned upside down. Men dressed and acted like women, while women switched roles with men. Children took on the roles of important adults, such as bishops or political leaders. A poor man was chosen to be "the Lord of Misrule." He led the celebration, while everyone else acted as his subjects.[10] To continue these switched roles, poor people went to the homes of the rich and demanded food and drink. If the poor did not get what they wanted, they pulled pranks or did other

Christmas was to replace the pagan winter celebrations that were taking place around December 25. Archaeologists believe England's Stonehenge served as a religious and astronomical center for tribal ceremonies linked to the winter and summer solstices.

mischief against the wealthy.[11] Although this practice sounds a lot like trick-or-treating on Halloween, it is an early example of people giving food and gifts to those who were less fortunate. A Frenchman who traveled in England during the late seventeenth century wrote that "they are not so much presents from friend to friend, or from equal to equal . . . as from superior to inferior."[12]

Oliver Cromwell and the Puritans

During the 1600s, a wave of religious reform swept over England. The British king was removed from the throne and the country was led by a man named Oliver Cromwell. Cromwell was a member of a religious group called the Puritans. The Puritans believed that excessive eating, drinking, and partying were sinful. They wanted to cleanse, or "purify," their church.[13] As part of their effort to make English society more religious, they made Christmas illegal. Anyone caught singing Christmas songs or taking part in any Christmas celebration could be arrested, fined, and even put in jail. Cromwell believed that "Christmas should be a sober day of reflection. Unless it fell on a Sunday, it should be treated no differently than any other day of the week. People should go about their daily activities, do their work, and go home to quietly consider what Christ means in their lives. No gifts should be given, no toasts made, and no carols sung. It was to be a solemn, colorless day."[14]

In England, Puritan rule did not last long. After Cromwell died his son took over, but the British people demanded a return of the monarchy. In 1660, Charles II returned to the British throne, and the celebration of Christmas went back on the calendar.

Things were different in North America, though. In 1620, a group of people left England and settled in what is now Plymouth, Massachusetts. This group was known as the Pilgrims, and they were part of the Puritan movement.[15] Soon after the Pilgrims landed in Massachusetts, they banned the Christmas holiday. Plymouth Colony's governor, William Bradford, did not mind if the Pilgrims celebrated

William Bradford (1590–1657)

Born in Austerfield, England, William Bradford became a member of the Separatists, a group of people who did not agree with the beliefs of the Church of England. He fled from England with other Separatists who were seeking religious freedom, first to Holland in 1608, and later to America. These Separatists are known today as the Pilgrims who landed on Plymouth Rock.

Once in America, Bradford became the second governor of Plymouth Colony after the death of John Carver, the first governor. He arranged the first Thanksgiving in 1621 and helped to maintain a relatively peaceful relationship with the neighboring American-Indian tribes. Bradford's book, known today as *History of Plymouth Plantation*, is the main source of information on Pilgrim life.

the religious aspects of Christmas. What he did not want was people going out "gaming and reveling in the streets."[16]

In New England, businesses and schools opened as usual on Christmas Day, and there was no celebrating allowed. From 1659 until 1681, Christmas was actually outlawed in the city of Boston. Anyone who showed Christmas spirit was fined five shillings.[17]

Things were different in the Southern colonies. Captain John Smith of the Jamestown settlement in Virginia wrote that he and his neighbors enjoyed Christmas, and the day "passed without incident."[18] In fact, the Pilgrims' beliefs did not play a role in any of the American colonies outside of New England.

Christmas Becomes a Holiday

Not everyone agreed with the Pilgrims' strict beliefs. As more and more settlers came from England, Holland, and other parts of Europe, their wishes overcame the Pilgrims' rules and traditions. In some places, the disorder and revelry that accompanied Christmas during this time became a serious problem. In 1828, the New York City Council had a special meeting to discuss the problem of gang violence and the drunken "Lords of

Disorder" who took over the streets on December 25. Soon a special police force patrolled the streets of New York on Christmas Day to protect citizens and their property.[19]

Despite local incidents of violence, the celebration of Christmas spread. The day finally became an official federal holiday in 1870.

The Changing Traditions of Christmas

During the 1800s, two important writers—one American and one British—changed the face of Christmas forever.

In 1819, American author Washington Irving published *The Sketchbook of Geoffrey Crayon.* The book told a series of stories about how the people of an English manor house celebrated Christmas. The stories described a British nobleman who invited peasants into his house for the holiday. The characters enjoyed customs dating from the Middle Ages, such as the crowning of a "Lord of Misrule." Both the upper and lower classes in the book enjoyed each other's company. The book showed Irving's belief that "Christmas should be a peaceful, warm-hearted holiday bringing groups together across lines of wealth or social status."[20] Although Irving's book read as though he were describing actual people and customs, most people

Left: A scene from Charles Dickens' *A Christmas Carol,* **where the grouchy Ebenezer Scrooge is visited by the ghost of his former business partner, Jacob Marley. Scrooge was not the only one who was changed for the better by what happened to him. The novel's heart-warming message of giving and love for all deeply affected its readers as well.**

today agree that Irving actually invented these events. Irving, however, would not admit he had made up the traditions described in his book. George William Curtis, a writer at the popular *Harper's* magazine, noted, "When Irving was reproached for describing an English Christmas which he had never seen, he replied that, although everything that he had described might not be seen at any single house, yet all of it could be seen somewhere in England, at Christmas."[21]

In 1843, another book was published that deeply affected people's perceptions of Christmas. British author Charles Dickens published his classic story, *A Christmas Carol.* The story's main character is Ebenezer Scrooge, a rich man who refuses to help the poor and who hates everything to do with Christmas. One Christmas Eve, he is visited by the ghosts of Christmas Past, Christmas Present, and Christmas Future. Through their eyes, and through Scrooge's relationship with his poor clerk, Bob Cratchit, and Cratchit's disabled son, Tiny Tim, Scrooge's entire outlook on Christmas changes. Scrooge—and the reader—learns that charity and goodwill toward all people are the greatest gifts anyone can give. *A Christmas Carol* became a sensation, both in England and in America, and changed the way people thought of the holiday.

American Traditions

During the 1800s, Americans began to shape their own Christmas traditions. Many of these—such as decorating evergreen trees, hanging wreaths, giving gifts, and sharing a festive meal—were actually taken from ancient traditions. Others, such as the figure of Santa Claus, came from other cultures and were adapted to fit American life. Christmas became a family holiday and a time of charity and generosity.

In addition, religious traditions became a bigger part of Christmas celebrations. A wave of immigrants during the mid-1800s through the early 1900s brought a large population of Irish, Italian, Polish, German, and other ethnic groups to

Washington Irving (1783–1859)

Although he is best known for his writing, throughout his life Washington Irving also worked as a lawyer, businessman, and a United States diplomat to both England and Spain. His most famous works are the short stories "Rip Van Winkle" and "The Legend of Sleepy Hollow." Irving played an important role in the history of American literature, as he is one of the first writers to earn fame and admiration both in the United States and in Europe.

Charles Dickens (1812–1870)

Charles Dickens was an Englishman whose numerous classic novels have made him one of the most famous writers of all time. He was known for his abilities to identify with young children, champion the poor, and denounce the tightfisted rich in his writing. In addition to *A Christmas Carol*, Dickens wrote four other Christmas stories. Some of his other renowned works include *Oliver Twist*, *David Copperfield*, *Great Expectations*, and *A Tale of Two Cities*.

America. These groups followed the Catholic faith and incorporated their religious beliefs and traditions to help create an American Christmas that included many religious aspects.[22]

Giving Gifts

One of the most important features of an American Christmas is giving gifts. Most people today believe that the practice of giving gifts began at Jesus' birth, when his family was visited by three kings (also called the Three Wise Men). These men brought symbolic gifts for the new baby—gold (a symbol of kingship), frankincense (a spice that symbolizes worship), and myrrh (a resin used to prepare bodies for burial).[23] After Clement Clarke Moore's poem, "An Account of a Visit from St. Nicholas" popularized the idea of Santa Claus, the focus of gift giving shifted to children. This new focus happened at the same time Christmas became more family oriented and less of an occasion to party.

Stores were advertising Christmas gifts as early as 1820. During the 1840s, most major newspapers had special advertising sections displaying Christmas gifts.[24] America became the center of the gift-giving tradition in the years after the Civil War. By 1900, mail-order catalogs and department stores relied on Christmas shopping for most of their sales.[25]

Christmas gifts during the 1800s and early 1900s were usually a far cry from the gifts we think of today. Most children received a few pieces of candy or fruit such as an orange—a real treat in the days before refrigeration and mass transportation made it possible for people to enjoy fresh fruit all year.[26] Clothes and homemade toys or dolls were also common gifts. This was especially true in rural areas without large department stores. *A Foxfire Christmas* is a collection of reminiscences from Appalachia, a rural area in the eastern United States. In it, people who grew up during the 1930s and 1940s recall family members creating corn-and-rag dolls as homemade copies of the expensive china dolls found in stores. Any child who actually received a store-bought doll remembered the gift with delight.[27] Even children in middle-class households did not always receive lavish gifts. Elizabeth Cady Stanton, who grew up to be an important figure in women's struggle for the right to vote, recalled one Christmas stocking filled with "a little paper of candy, one of raisins, another of nuts, a red apple, an *olie-koek* [cookie], and a bright silver quarter of a dollar in the toe."[28]

This 19th century portrayal of Father Christmas carrying a basket full of toys for good children is very different from the reality of that time. Most children found a few pieces of candy, fruit, or homemade toys in their stockings or under their trees.

Elizabeth Cady Stanton (1815–1902)

Elizabeth Cady Stanton helped to establish the women's rights movement in the United States. In 1848, she and Lucretia Mott organized the nation's first women's rights convention in Seneca Falls, New York. At the convention, Stanton wrote a Declaration of Sentiments, modeled after the Declaration of Independence. Stanton also wanted woman suffrage, or the right for women to vote.

Stanton worked with abolitionists during the Civil War. In 1869, she and Susan B. Anthony established the National Woman Suffrage Association, of which she was president until 1890. Stanton's hard work eventually led to the approval of the nineteenth Amendment in 1920.

It was not until the mid-1900s, when mass production made toys cheaper and more readily available, that manufactured toys, games, and bikes became popular Christmas gifts.

Although Christmas today is primarily a commercial holiday, it is still a celebration rich with many historical and cultural traditions.

3

The Cultural Significance of Christmas

Christmas has major cultural significance, both in the United States and in the rest of the world. The day has become a blend of religion, folklore, and commercial excess.

The Role of Religion

The day is first and foremost a religious holiday. Historian Penne L. Restad notes that "Of all holidays, Christmas was a perfect agency for transporting religion and religious feelings into the home and for righting the excesses and failures of the public world. . . . The festival focused on the very essence of Christian home sentiment that venerated Jesus and honored children."[1]

Many families incorporate Mass or church services as part of their Christmas celebrations. Even people who do not attend church regularly often go to services on Christmas. Christmas Masses in the Catholic church can be quite elaborate. Choirs sing Christmas hymns, there is a grand procession, and the story of Jesus' birth is retold. Many churches, both Catholic and Protestant, hold Christmas pageants. At these pageants, children dress up as major figures in the Christmas story and reenact the events surrounding Jesus' birth. These pageants usually include readings from the Bible and the singing of religious hymns.

Advent

Christmas became such an important religious event that Christian churches created a period of preparation. The four weeks before Christmas are called Advent, and they are a time for people to become spiritually ready to accept Jesus into their lives.

The Advent wreath symbolizes the coming of Jesus Christ. Each of the four candles has a special meaning. Some people choose to have all the candles the same color.

Advent comes from a Latin word that means "the coming." The season was officially established by church leaders during the sixth century.[2] Advent traditions spread quickly throughout Christian Europe because they gave people a distinct way to remember and celebrate.

Among observant Christians, the most well-known and distinctive feature of the season is the Advent wreath. This wreath includes four candles, one for each of the four Sundays before Christmas. The candles for the first, second, and fourth Sundays are purple. They symbolize three precious gifts of Christmas. These gifts are hope, peace, and love. The candle for the third week is pink. It symbolizes the joy of new life. A new candle is lit during Mass or church service on each of the four Sundays before Christmas, and the Bible readings during this time stress preparation for Jesus' coming. Many Christians also have Advent wreaths in their homes. They light a candle every Sunday and read a short prayer.

Folklore and Cultural Traditions

Many countries around the world have a strong Catholic background. Countries such as Brazil, Mexico, Spain, and Italy celebrate Christmas as an important Catholic holiday. These countries, along with many others, also tie the holiday to their own folklore.

The character of Babushka in Russia is a good example of how a figure from traditional folklore has become part of a country's Christmas traditions. "Babushka" is the Russian word for "grandmother." In the folktale, an old woman named Babushka was visited by the Three Wise Men. They were on their way to visit the newborn baby Jesus and invited Babushka to come along. The old woman refused to go because of the cold weather, but as soon as the travelers left, she changed her mind. Quickly, Babushka filled a basket with gifts and set out after the Wise Men. However, she had waited too long and never found them. To this day, she is still on her journey and still searching to find the baby Jesus. Babushka leaves gifts for all the children just in case one of them is Jesus, so Russian children expect to receive gifts from Babushka at Christmas.[3] The Italians have a similar story, featuring an old woman named "Befana."[4] These characters echo many of the elements of the Santa Claus story, but come from traditional ethnic folklore.

La Befana

While Italy now has Santa Claus (called Babbo Natale), there was a time when the primary giver of gifts was an ugly old woman called La Befana. La Befana came on the night of January 5, the eve of the Epiphany. The Epiphany was the day that the Three Kings arrived at the manger to give the baby Jesus his gifts.

Legend has it that La Befana was an old lady who enjoyed cooking and cleaning. One day, the Three Kings stopped by her house while on the way to see Jesus. They asked La Befana if she would like to join them, but she declined, saying that she was too busy. Soon after they left, she reconsidered and ran out of the house with a bag of treats and her broom. La Befana could not find the Three Kings, but divine power enabled her to fly on her broom. Now, every year on the eve of the Epiphany, La Befana flies from house to house, searching for the baby Jesus. She leaves gifts for the children in every house, and coal for those who are bad.

In 2005, a woman dressed up as La Befana, a witch Italian children believe gives them presents, at St. Peter's Square at the Vatican.

The Commercial Side of Christmas

Religion and folklore are certainly significant parts of Christmas, but in recent years, the commercial aspects of the holiday have become increasingly important and obvious.

Shopping for Christmas presents goes back to the 1820s. With each passing year, stores stocked more and more items during the Christmas season. Most gifts were aimed at children. An 1865 illustration in *Harper's Monthly Magazine* shows the variety of new merchandise available for children. The illustration included "an inexpensive pocket watch, a teething ring, a china doll and a neat doll carriage, picture books, a woolly lamb on wheels, an easel and boxed paint set, a fully equipped tool chest, a drum, and a sword. For the adult members of the household, the presents are sparser. There is a pile of gift books on a table. Father has a pipe and Mother has a perfume bottle."[5]

In earlier days, most Christmas shopping was done on Christmas Eve. In her description of life in London, England, during the 1870s, M. Vivian Hughes noted, "Nowadays it is difficult to realize that no Christmas preparations were made until the week before the day itself. . . . Christmas Eve

Shoppers crowd Fourteenth Street in New York City in 1899. The 19th century saw the commercialization of Christmas with stores and manufacturers marketing the majority of their products to children.

was the day we liked best. My father came home early, laden with parcels."[6]

By 1900, however, the Christmas season had stretched to two weeks before Christmas. Stores and manufacturers used this extra time to advertise and sell their products. During World War II, which was fought between 1939 and 1945, people had to shop and mail their packages earlier so that the presents would get to soldiers stationed far away in Europe and Asia in time for the holiday. This extended the shopping season even further. Stores began putting up holiday displays immediately after Thanksgiving. Today, Christmas displays seem to appear right after Halloween, almost two months before Christmas!

Today, shoppers in the United States spend billions of dollars during the holiday season. The average person in the United States spent more than a thousand dollars on Christmas gifts in 2002.[7]

The commercialism of Christmas has always angered religious leaders. People criticized the commercialism of Christmas as early as the fifth century. Many people feel that the true meaning of Christmas—a celebration of Jesus' birth—has been forgotten and Christmas is now just an excuse to spend money and acquire more material things. In 1993, twenty-five religious leaders signed a statement protesting the commercialization of Christmas. The statement said that "Consumption has taken on an almost religious quality; malls have become the new shrines of worship."[8] It went on to say "Christmas giving, in all its forms, is enriched when spiritual and ethical values overshadow the almost chronic compulsions to buy. . . . We call on all people of faith to speak out against the overcommercialism of Christmas in our media and malls. . . . Christmas was never intended to be a crass marketing ploy. Let us restore the spiritual and life-affirming potential of the season—and take it into the new year."[9]

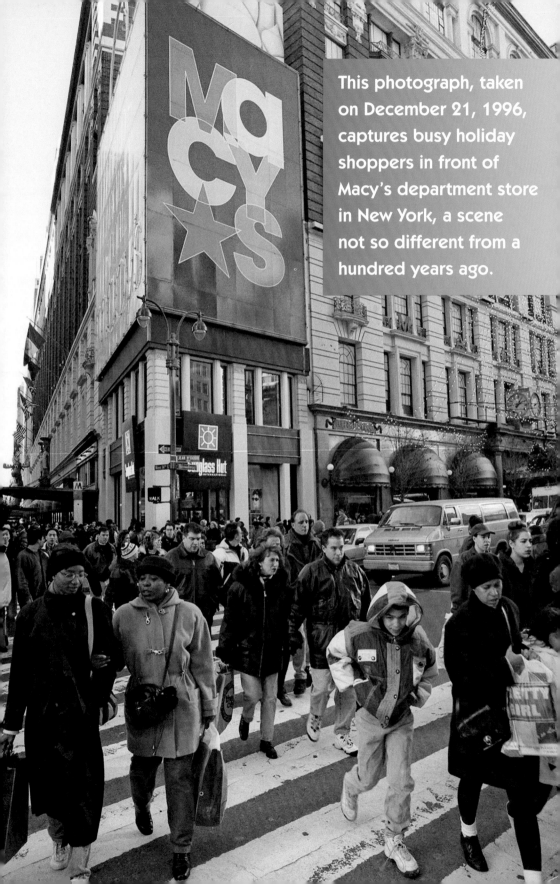

This photograph, taken on December 21, 1996, captures busy holiday shoppers in front of Macy's department store in New York, a scene not so different from a hundred years ago.

Who Celebrates Christmas?

Christmas is celebrated by people all over the world. Although people of all ages take part in Christmas celebrations, for the past 150 years or so, the celebrations have focused mainly on children.

Santa and Children

Before the 1800s, children were not the focus of gift giving at Christmas. During the Middle Ages, adults exchanged gifts. The upper classes usually gave food, drink, and money to the poor.

During the 1800s, Christmas became more of a family holiday. All members of a family would give gifts to each other. Then a poem written by a New York professor introduced a new aspect to gift giving and changed the focus of Christmas forever.

Clement Clarke Moore was both a bishop at an Episcopal church in New York City and a professor at the General Theological Seminary. In 1822, he wrote a poem for his three daughters, called "An Account of a Visit from St. Nicholas."[1] His story was taken up by the Dutch who settled New York City. St. Nicholas became the patron saint of New York City, and Dutch families there followed the practice of giving gifts to children. The Dutch called St. Nicholas "Sinterklaas," which was later Americanized to "Santa Claus."[2] The Dutch celebrated St. Nicholas' Day on December 6. Clement Moore's poem was the first instance where St. Nicholas was tied into the Christmas holiday.

Moore had written his poem simply to entertain his children. He never intended for it to be published. Then a friend who was visiting the family enjoyed the poem so much that she secretly copied it down and submitted it to a newspaper in Troy, New York. The following year, the *Troy Sentinel* published the poem, which instantly became a Christmas classic.[3] Today, Moore's poem

Clement Clarke Moore's poem "An Account of a Visit from St. Nicholas," was the first time St. Nicholas was associated with Christmas. St. Nicholas eventually evolved into Santa Claus, and this picture illustrates the childhood wish to catch a glimpse of the jolly old man who slides down the chimney to deliver presents on Christmas Eve.

is known as "A Visit from Saint Nicholas" or "'Twas the Night Before Christmas."

In the 1880s, Thomas Nast illustrated Moore's poem for *Harper's* magazine. Every year, Nast added details to his pictures of Santa. Author and Christmas historian Ace Collins explains Nast's influence: "He enhanced the legend of Santa Claus and fleshed out the life of the man who was filling stockings from coast to coast. Nast drew Santa's workshop, created the 'naughty and nice' list, and, in 1885, sketched the home of the man in red."[4]

Moore's Santa Claus comes to the narrator's house just to give gifts to children. This tradition took hold and grew over the years. Author Penne Restad notes that "Children remained largely the recipients of gifts, although trading among themselves and even giving presents to parents was not unknown. . . . Parents, of course, usually gave much more to their children than they received."[5]

Children and parents also exchanged gifts in other countries. In 1835, a writer named George Ticknor visited Dresden, Germany, where he was delighted by the custom of family members exchanging gifts at Christmas. Ticknor wrote:

> We witnessed some of this very peculiar national feeling and custom; that, I mean, of the children giving presents to the parents and the parents to the children on Christmas Eve. . . . The presents which the children had

George Ticknor (1791–1871)

Born in Boston, Massachusetts, George Ticknor was a renowned educator and author. Ticknor attended Dartmouth College and briefly practiced law in Boston. He then studied at the University of Göttingen in Germany for two years. In 1817, Ticknor was offered the newly created position of Smith professor of French and Spanish languages and literatures, and professor of *belles-lettres* at Harvard University in Boston.

In 1835, he resigned from the position, which was then filled by Henry Wadsworth Longfellow. During the course of his life, Ticknor was involved in many ventures, including his work as co-founder of the Boston Public Library.

secretly prepared for the elder members of the family were placed under the tree. . . . There was nothing very valuable or beautiful in what was given, yet it was all received with so much pleasure by the parents and elder brother, that the children were delighted, and kissed us all round very heartily.[6]

Christmas Around the World

People all over the world celebrate Christmas, and every country and culture has its own local traditions.

Many countries begin the Christmas season with a special feast day or celebration several weeks before Christmas Day. In Sweden and other Scandinavian countries, the Christmas season officially starts on December 13, which is the feast of Santa Lucia, or Saint Lucy. This day is sometimes called "little Yule" and celebrates light. Traditionally, the oldest daughter in a family dresses in a long white gown with a red sash and wears a crown made of twigs that holds nine lit candles.[7] The family sings songs to honor Saint Lucy and eats a special breakfast by candlelight. The breakfast includes pinwheel-shaped rolls called "lussekatter."[8]

Mexico also begins its celebrations before Christmas Day. On December 16, children take

A reenactment of Mary and Joseph's search for shelter, called La Gran Posada, takes place in San Antonio, Texas, where the procession travels downtown to the nation's oldest Catholic sanctuary, the San Jose Cathedral.

Saint Lucy

Saint Lucy is the patron saint of the blind and those with eye trouble. While the exact details of her life and death are unclear, we know that Lucy was a martyr who lived in the city of Syracuse on Sicily.

Legend has it that Lucy lived in the early fourth century—during the rule of Diocletian—when Christians were viciously persecuted, or tortured for their beliefs. Lucy promised her life to Christ, much like a nun. Her mother attempted to arrange a marriage between Lucy and a pagan—a person who believes in many gods. Lucy wanted to convince her mother that a life devoted to Christ was worthwhile, so she took her to the tomb of Saint Agatha. There, an illness that her mother had been suffering from for several years was miraculously cured through prayer.

Her mother realized that Lucy's chosen path was worthy, but the man who Lucy was supposed to marry became enraged. He went to the governor and told him that Lucy was a Christian. The governor tried to shame Lucy, but the power of God prevented him from doing so. Eventually, Lucy was brutally murdered. While the specifics of her death are uncertain, legend has it that Lucy's eyes were taken as part of the torture, but God returned them. Lucy's bravery and loyalty to God spread throughout the Christian world and earned her sainthood.

In Stockholm, Sweden, this girl portrays Saint Lucy "Queen of Lights" as her maidens light the crown of candles upon her head. On December 13, Swedish tradition has young girls dress up as Saint Lucy to celebrate light during the darkest time of the year, a time close to the winter solstice.

part in a procession called "las posadas." This procession reenacts Mary and Joseph's journey as they looked for a place to stay in Bethlehem before Jesus' birth. Two children carry small statues of Mary and Joseph and lead a parade through town. The group goes from house to house, seeking "posada," or shelter. The procession is repeated every day until Christmas Eve. On that night, children put a figure of baby Jesus into the Nativity scene in the local church and then attend midnight Mass.[9]

Celebrations can also extend past Christmas Day. January 6 is the Epiphany, or the Feast of the Three Kings. In Spain and Latin American countries, this day is a bigger feast day than Christmas. Families exchange gifts on this day to remember the gifts that the Three Kings brought to Jesus.

British Traditions

Great Britain has many of the same Christmas traditions as the United States. This country, however, does have some unique traditions as well. People enjoy pulling "crackers," which are small, brightly wrapped tubes. When you pull on either end, the boxes pop open with a cracking sound and

These crackers hold small toys or other goodies.

a small prize, such as a toy or a piece of jewelry, falls out.

The British also enjoy a special Christmas food called plum pudding. Plum pudding does not contain plums and is not a sweet, creamy dessert, as Americans think of this food. Plum pudding dates back to the Middle Ages and includes suet (a kind of fat), flour, sugar, raisins, nuts, and spices. The ingredients are tied in a cloth and boiled until the mixture becomes "plum" or puffs up to fill the

A 19th century work, called *Hurrah for the Christmas Pudding,* depicts the Christmas dish also known as plum pudding.

cloth. Then the pudding is sliced like a cake, topped with cream, and eaten.[10] Often, one slice of pudding contains a coin, a ring, or some other small prize.

In Great Britain, Canada, and Australia, the day after Christmas is called Boxing Day. This tradition began during the Middle Ages, when churches would open boxes filled with donated money and give it to the poor.[11] Later, December 26 became the day when people gave boxes of gifts to their servants or to tradespeople, such as bakers or butchers.[12] The day after Christmas was chosen for this exchange because Christmas was a day to spend with family and was too hectic for an additional exchange of gifts.[13] Today, the tradition continues, and December 26 is a day when British people give gifts to people who work for them or perform a service, such as delivering the mail or taking away the trash. This is another example of spreading Christmas cheer to a large number of people, so everyone can share in the holiday traditions.

Symbols of Christmas

F ew holidays have as many well-known symbols as Christmas does. From the relatively modern Santa Claus and his reindeer to ancient symbols such as wreaths and Nativity scenes, many objects have become powerful images of Christmas.

Santa Claus

Today, Santa Claus is a large, jolly figure with a long white beard who flies around the world on Christmas Eve and gives out toys to all the good children in the world. But Santa's origins have little to do with his modern image. The figure of Santa Claus was originally based on a real person named Saint Nicholas.

Saint Nicholas was a bishop who lived in what is now Turkey during the fourth century A.D. Saint Nicholas was a very generous man who enjoyed helping the poor, often in secret. He became known for giving money and gifts to poor families, and also as a protector of children.

Saint Nicholas's legend spread around the world, eventually coming to New York City with Dutch settlers during the 1600s. His present-day appearance as a red-suited man with toys on his back comes from the poem "A Visit from Saint Nicholas" by Clement Clarke Moore.

Parents, teachers, and other adult authority figures soon took advantage of the idea that Santa

Right: The legendary Santa Claus was based on a bishop named Saint Nicholas who lived during the fourth century A.D. and gave money and gifts to the poor. Clement Clarke Moore's poem, "A Visit from Saint Nicholas," gave rise to Santa's modern-day image of a jolly, bearded man in a red suit.

A Merry Christmas

Christians often brought evergreens into their homes to remind them of the eternal life promised by Jesus.[4]

Martin Luther, a religious reformer who lived during the 1500s, is credited with being the first person to add lights to a Christmas tree. The story goes that as Luther walked home one night, he was awed by the brilliant stars twinkling in the sky through the evergreen trees. To recapture the scene, he put up a tree inside his house and attached lit candles to its branches.[5]

German immigrants brought the Christmas tree tradition to America during the 1830s. Americans, however, found this practice strange because it seemed to honor an object from nature, rather than a religious figure. That changed in 1846, when magazines published pictures of Great Britain's Queen Victoria and her family gathered around a Christmas tree. Queen Victoria's husband was German and had brought the Christmas tree custom to the royal family. Since Queen Victoria was very popular, both in England and the United States, the general public rushed to copy this Christmas decoration.[6]

Christmas trees were decorated with many different things. During the 1890s, ornaments were imported from Germany. People also hung

Left: Sixteenth century Germans were the first to decorate evergreen trees for Christmas. Great Britain's Queen Victoria adopted the practice, and soon, the masses in both England and America began to do the same.

foods such as popcorn, berries, apples, nuts, and cookies. The invention of electricity meant that Christmas lights replaced candles, making things much safer and more convenient.

Wreaths

Like evergreen trees, evergreen wreaths were also an ancient symbol of eternal life, both because of their color and also because of their circular shape. Many families hang wreaths on their front doors or porches. Today, wreaths are usually decorated with bows and small ornaments.

Poinsettias

A poinsettia is a red-and-green plant that comes from Mexico. It was probably first grown by the ancient Aztecs, who called the plant "cuetlaxochitle." The Aztecs admired its beauty so much that they considered the plant sacred.[7]

During the holiday season, you will see many decorative wreaths hanging on front doors.

Much later, the plant became part of a Spanish legend that gave the flower its first connection with the Nativity. This legend said that a poor Mexican girl named Pepita was sad because she had no gift to bring to the baby Jesus in a Nativity scene at a local church. The townspeople told Pepita any gift was worthy if it was given with love. Pepita picked some green weeds and offered the ordinary-looking plants to Jesus. Suddenly, the weeds changed to bright red. Everyone believed they had seen a miracle. Now the plant had a new name: "*flor de nochebuena*," or "flower of the blessed night."[8]

The plant received the name we know it by today because of an American named Joel Poinsett. Poinsett served as the United States ambassador to Mexico. In the 1820s, he brought some seeds from a *flor de nochebuena* back to the United States.

A Spanish legend gave this flower the name "flor de nochebuena" (flower of the blessed night). It was renamed the poinsettia after the United States ambassador to Mexico, Joel Poinsett.

Poinsett grew the plant and marketed it to florists. They began selling the plant as a Christmas flower because of its red and green colors, and it became known as the poinsettia, after Poinsett.[9]

Mistletoe

Mistletoe is another Christmas tradition that has ancient beginnings. The ancient Celts believed the plant had magical qualities because it flowered during the winter, and also because it grew in the tops of trees rather than being rooted to the ground.[10] The Celts hung bits of mistletoe in their homes for good luck. In time, the plant became a symbol of love. If a couple passed under the mistletoe, they had to kiss.

Historians say that the Druids cut the mistletoe that grew on the sacred oak and gave it to the people for charms.

Christians in Great Britain first saw mistletoe as a religious symbol during the 1840s. They believed that just as Jesus brought life to the world after he was crucified, mistletoe brought life during the dead, barren days of winter. Ace Collins writes that "Christians across Europe seized upon the religious symbolism of mistletoe and . . . posted the plant over their doors . . . to show the world that they believed in the love God had sent the world through his Son, Jesus Christ."[11]

Mistletoe decorated with a ribbon is often hung in doorways during the Christmas season.

Christmas Stockings

Children all over the world hang stockings near the fireplace on Christmas Eve so that Santa Claus will fill them with gifts. This custom is closely tied to a legend about Saint Nicholas. The legend says that when he heard about a family who was too poor to pay the dowry (a marriage gift) for their daughter, Nicholas climbed onto their roof one night and dropped a bag of gold down the chimney. The gold landed in the girl's stocking, which she had put by the fireplace to dry. This story grew into the belief

Colorful Christmas stockings are both decorative and functional.

that Santa came down the chimney to leave gifts in children's stockings.[12]

In the past, most of a child's Christmas gifts were left in actual stockings. As gifts became larger and more elaborate, they were left under the tree, but small gifts, such as candy or money, were still placed in the stocking. Families also began to hang large Christmas stockings, often printed with holiday designs, as well as the recipient's name, rather than hanging actual socks and tights.

Nativity Scenes

The story of the Nativity is the central tradition of Christmas. In 1223, an Italian priest named St.

Francis of Assisi wanted to create a simple way to explain Jesus' birth to the uneducated people he ministered to. He built a crude nativity out of wood and in order to conduct a nativity scene, he had local people play the parts of Mary, Joseph, and the shepherds.[13]

Nativity scenes became popular around the world and were often part of elaborate Christmas pageants featuring songs and processions. After World War I (1914–1918), churches and public buildings began to display Nativities. During the 1950s, businesses began selling scenes people could place in their yards.[14] Some displays, called "Living Nativities," even featured live animals. People also

Displaying Nativity scenes in yards and under Christmas trees is a popular tradition, but this custom had more humble origins.

placed smaller Nativity scenes inside their houses, often on the mantelpiece above the fireplace or underneath the Christmas tree. Nativities often include angels, which are an important part of the Biblical story of the Nativity and have also become a popular symbol of Christmas.

In recent years, however, Nativities have been the subject of controversy. While most people do not object to a church displaying religious symbols, many feel that a display in a public area, such as a downtown square, a public school, or government building, is a violation of the separation of church and state, which is protected by the First Amendment. Some people feel that displaying a Nativity elevates the Christian faith above other religions, which is against the U.S. Constitution. "If there's one thing the First Amendment does is it prohibits any government or government agency—public schools are government agencies—from elevating one faith above another," Bruce Prescott, executive director of Mainstream Baptists of Oklahoma, told FOX News in 2004.[15] That year, FOX News reported several communities where Nativities and other Christmas displays were the subject of lawsuits or taken down altogether.[16]

Many people support the separation of church and state and do not want to see one particular faith promoted by the government. Cliff Walker, the publisher of *Positive Atheism* magazine, has written that "When governments allow themselves to endorse religion at all, the tendency has always been for the dominant religious viewpoint to get all the endorsements and for other viewpoints to be left out . . . Our founders crafted the first godless constitution in the world. . . . The founders were painfully aware of the persecutions inevitably practiced when religion is established by government."[17] Walker goes on to say that "the only way to ensure fairness is to agree that promoting religion is not the role of government. . . . True religious liberty occurs only when we agree to keep our government's hands out of religious messages and ritual at all levels—even something as seemingly innocuous as a holiday display."[18]

Religious organizations and many ordinary citizens have a different perspective. People with these beliefs are fighting these bans. "The Supreme Court has never declared nativity scenes, the singing of Christmas carols, and other traditional Christmas celebrations unconstitutional," says Joshua Carden, an attorney with the Christian legal defense organization the Alliance for Defense

Fund.[19] John W. Whitehead, president of a free-speech group called the Rutherford Institute, agrees, saying "I think the businesses and the schools have just gone too far. . . . It's supposed to be a time of peace and freedom and fun. And they've kind of made it into a . . . kind of gray day."[20]

Christmas Carols

Christmas carols began in England during the Middle Ages. Wandering musicians traveled from town to town, visiting castles and other estates. After they sang songs of the season, they hoped to receive money or a hot meal in return.[21]

During the 1800s, Christmas trees became popular because Queen Victoria and Prince Albert of Great Britain had one. The royal couple was also responsible for the popularity of Christmas carols. Prince Albert enjoyed singing, and the royal family always included Christmas songs as part of their holiday celebrations. To please the queen, groups of carolers began coming to her castle in London and singing outside the gates. These groups often made their way through the city streets afterward, continuing to spread Christmas joy through music to passersby.[22]

This tradition continues today. During the Christmas season, groups of carolers can sometimes be seen singing on street corners in a town's business district or walking through neighborhoods. These groups often accept donations for charity, and they might also receive small treats such as hot chocolate or cookies from appreciative listeners. Other carolers take part in church services or perform at hospitals, nursing homes, and other places where people might be spending a lonely or unhappy Christmas.

Carols cover many different aspects of the Christmas celebration. Some are religious. "Silent Night," "Angels We Have Heard on High," and "Away in a Manger" describe the night Jesus was born. Other carols have a different theme. "Deck the Halls" and "Silver Bells" describe specific delights of the Christmas season. "Santa Claus is Coming to Town" and "Frosty the Snowman" present a more modern, nonreligious picture of holiday cheer. Many of today's familiar carols were collected by noted British composer Ralph Vaughn Williams and British music teacher and folksong collector Cecil Sharp. These men had a great deal to do with keeping carols alive and introducing them to mass audiences during the 19th and 20th centuries.

In Jersey City, New Jersey, a Christmas tree and nativity scene are installed in front of city hall after the court overturned a ruling that claimed displaying religious symbols on public property was unconstitutional. Secular symbols such as Santa Claus and Frosty the Snowman were also displayed.

One of the most beloved Christmas carols is "Rudolph the Red-Nosed Reindeer." This bright-nosed reindeer was not part of the original group of eight reindeer described by Clement Clarke Moore in "A Visit from Saint Nicholas." Instead, Rudolph was invented more than one hundred years later by a writer at a department store. In 1939, Robert L. May wrote the poem to bring more customers into the Montgomery Ward store where he worked. May invented the story of a red-nosed reindeer who is laughed at until his bright nose makes it possible for Santa to deliver his gifts on a foggy Christmas Eve. The store sold more than 2 million copies of the poem that Christmas season, and more than 3 million when it was reissued in 1946. In 1949, May's friend, songwriter Johnny Marks, wrote a song based on May's poem. The song was recorded by cowboy singing star Gene Autry and became a huge hit. The song has been the inspiration for books and television specials, and it is still one of the most popular Christmas carols today.[23]

Christmas Cards

Like so many Christmas traditions, the idea of sending Christmas cards began in England. In 1843, John Calcott Horsley designed the first commercial Christmas card.[24] The card was small and did not fold open. In the center was a picture of a happy family. Smaller pictures of people helping the poor were placed on either side of the family portrait. "A Merry Christmas and a Happy New

"Rudolph the Red-Nosed Reindeer" may have started out as a simple gimmick to lure more customers into a department store. But the story of the little reindeer who went from outcast to hero has become almost as important to the holiday season as Santa Claus himself.

Year" was printed on top, with a space for the sender to sign the card on the bottom.[25]

The first American Christmas card appeared in the early 1850s. It was similar to British cards and showed small pictures of Santa, gifts, and food around a drawing of a family exchanging gifts. This card was more than just an expression of holiday cheer, In addition to wishing the recipient "A Merry Christmas and Happy New Year," it also included the name of a department story in Albany, New York.[26] Advertising was already beginning to creep into Christmas traditions.

Christmas cards gained in popularity in Great Britain between 1860 and 1880. They were not as widely used in the United States, however. This changed because of a German immigrant named Louis Prang, who moved to Boston in 1856 and opened a print shop. Around 1880, Prang started an annual competition for Christmas card designs. Well-known painters and magazine illustrators flooded Prang with spectacular paintings filled with bright colors and lavish details. Prang's cards became a sensation, and suddenly everyone wanted to send them.[27] The cards were much more elaborate than anything before or since, and included silk tassels; heavy, perfumed paper; feathers; and even bits of sparkling glass embedded in the paper. These works of art were often framed or displayed on tabletops.[28]

Prang's success encouraged other printers to enter the market. By 1890, many other companies were printing and selling Christmas cards. Many were German or British. Prang said that low wages and cheaper materials used by other companies "made it impossible to battle successfully against foreign competition in the same line" and closed his business.[29]

In the late 1800s, German print shop owner Louis Prang popularized Christmas cards in the United States with his elaborate designs.

The cards of the late 1800s usually featured family scenes, images of Santa, or pictures of children sledding or enjoying the holiday and the season. During the 1900s, cards began to have more religious imagery, including angels, churches, children praying, and the Nativity. According to Christmas historian Ace Collins, "Christmas cards became not only a tool for extending greetings to business associates, friends, and family but also a way to share the gospel with others."[30]

Today, millions of Christmas cards are sent each year. These cards come in a variety of designs, from religious to humorous, traditional to outrageous. The old themes of the Nativity, Santa, the winter season, and family togetherness are still the most popular. It is hard to imagine the Christmas season without cards arriving in the mail, bearing good wishes for Christmas and hope for a happy New Year.

Nutcracker

Wooden nutcrackers in the shapes of authority figures such as soldiers, knights, and kings have been around since the fifteenth century. Villagers in the Ore Mountains of Germany handcrafted these nutcrackers. They have become central to

Many people decorate their homes with nutcrackers around Christmas. This collection shows off a variety of old and new nutcrackers.

Christmas celebrations as well as subjects of stories.

One of the most famous nutcracker stories was originally written by E. T. A. Hoffman. This story was called *The Nutcracker and the Mouse King* and was not intended for children. Alexandre Dumas wrote an adaptation of Hoffman's original tale. Composer Peter Ilyich Tchaikovsky created a ballet from Dumas' adaptation.

The Nutcracker is a ballet about a girl named Clara who receives a nutcracker for Christmas from an uncle. Her brother is jealous and breaks the toy, but, the uncle is able to repair it. That night Clara is concerned about the nutcracker and goes to check on him. She falls asleep holding the doll. Clara is awakened at midnight by the sound of mice. When she tries to run away, the mice surround her. The Nutcracker rises up and leads his army to battle with the Mouse King. Clara throws her slipper at the Mouse King and the Nutcracker stabs him. The battle has ended with the death of the Mouse King and Clara's precious Nutcracker. She cries over him and her tears bring him back to life. At this point in the ballet, the Nutcracker becomes a prince and leads Clara to the land of the Sugar Plum Fairy where they dance and dance. At the end of the ballet, Clara wakes up with the Nutcracker in her arms.

There have been many versions of the Nutcracker tale. The ballet has become a Christmas tradition for many.

6

Christmas Today

Today, Christmas is the biggest and most popular holiday in the United States, Great Britain, and many other parts of the world. As they have for centuries, people celebrate by going to church and singing Christmas carols. They decorate their homes with wreaths, Christmas trees, Nativities, and other signs of the season. They hang stockings, place gifts under the tree, and send cards to family, friends, and business associates. Families and friends exchange gifts and share large meals.

Many people celebrate Christmas as a festive holiday without any religious connections. They exchange gifts and share meals and decorate their homes with Christmas trees, wreaths, and other symbols. They enjoy festive Christmas carols and watch Christmas-themed movies and television shows.

Many people celebrate Christmas as a festive holiday without any religious connections. They exchange gifts and share meals and decorate their homes with Christmas trees, wreaths, and other symbols. They enjoy festive Christmas carols and

Federal Holidays

Federal holidays are like vacation days for employees of the federal government. The President and Congress decide which days are to be selected as federal holidays. These holidays are then observed in the District of Columbia and by federal employees in all states. Each state's governor also has the right to decide which holidays his or her state will acknowledge.

Banks and schools are usually closed on federal holidays. If a federal holiday falls on a Saturday, it is usually observed on Friday, and if it falls on a Sunday, it is typically observed on Monday. Although there are several federal holidays that all states observe, many states have their own unique holidays.

Some families exchange gifts on Christmas.

watch Christmas-themed movies and television shows.

Christmas has been a federal holiday in the United States since 1870.[1] It is also an official holiday in many other countries around the world. Most businesses are closed on Christmas, and so are schools, banks, and government offices.

Has Christmas Become Too Commercial?

Ever since stores began selling Christmas gifts during the 1800s, people have complained that the holiday has become too commercial. Many stores make most of their earnings for the year in the four weeks between Thanksgiving and Christmas. The day after Thanksgiving is the official start of the Christmas season, and stores open at dawn to serve crowds of shoppers eager to buy the latest must-have items at the best price. These shopping scenes sometimes turn into chaos as people are trampled and fights break out over especially desirable items, such as the newest video game or computer.

Many people have spoken out against the commercial frenzy that has become such a big part of the Christmas season. "Christmas is a simple holiday," says Dr. Caron B. Goode. "It is a time of giving, but for many families this simplicity is overshadowed by the consuming side of Christmas. We rush to Christmas sales, and spend precious evening and weekend hours fervently trying to fulfill every Christmas wish. This relatively new and consumer driven tradition often renders us exhausted and anxious, which negatively affects our spirit of giving. The consuming side of Christmas also leaves us precious little time to spend with our families."[2]

Religious leaders also complain that the true meaning of Christmas has been lost in the race to spend the most money and acquire the best new toy. In 1993, the Center for the Study of

Busy Texans rush about in Highland Mall in Austin two days before Christmas. Many people believe Christmas has become too commercialized and the true meaning of the holiday has been lost.

Commercialism issued a statement saying that Christmas must be more than just spending money.[3]

People have also sought to cut back on commercialism in order to make Christmas a less hectic time. Several years ago, a group of Methodist churches started the "Hundred Dollar Holiday" program. Participants agreed to "limit the amount of money they spend on the holiday to a hundred dollars—to celebrate the holiday with a seventh or eighth of the normal American materialism."[4] Founder Bill McKibben recalls that the program's aim was not based on religion. "When we'd begun thinking about Hundred Dollar Holidays, it was mostly out of concern for the environment or for poor people. Think of all that wrapping paper, we said, all those batteries, all that plastic. Think of all the needy people who could be helped if we donated our money to them instead. Think of all those families who went deep into debt trying to have a 'proper' Christmas."[5] As he worked on the campaign, however, McKibben discovered that people responded for another reason. They "wanted a more joyous Christmas. We were feeling cheated—as if the season didn't bring with it the happiness we wanted. . . . Many of our friends, Christian or not, felt that too much of the chance

These three young boys are volunteers for Operation Blue
Santa, a police sponsored program that delivers Christmas
packages to low income families in Austin, Texas.

for family togetherness was being robbed by the pressures of Christmas busyness and the tensions of gift-giving. Christmas had become something to endure at least as much as it had become something to enjoy."[6]

The Hundred Dollar Holidays program, and others like it, encourage people to exchange homemade gifts. People cook baked goods and other food. They carve items out of wood or build household goods. They sew clothes or knit blankets. People also offer their time to others. A grandfather might record himself reading stories and give the tape to a grandchild. A teenager might make a book of coupons promising to baby-sit a sibling, help around the house, or even give a back rub. A mother might arrange treasured family photos into a scrapbook or a calendar. The possibilities are endless. These gifts allow people to help each other and share precious times without the pressures of going into debt.

Christmas Forever

Despite the commercialism, the true spirit of Christmas still exists today. Families and friends spend time together. People donate money, gifts, and time to charity to ensure that the less fortunate—especially children and families—can have a

On December 10, 2002, at New York's Kennedy Airport, volunteers participated in Operation Christmas Child, an international relief organization which airlifted over 80,000 gifts to children suffering from HIV/AIDS in Africa.

happy holiday. Others sing Christmas carols at hospitals, nursing homes, and community gatherings. These and many other Christmas traditions reflect the values taught by Jesus, as well as ancient traditions that shone light into a dark world. By celebrating and honoring elements from

Families decorate their homes for the holidays.

folklore, ancient cultures, and other religions, we incorporate Christmas rituals that come from simpler times and traditions.[7]

For many families, the Christmas season is a time of beloved traditions. Families enjoy special foods and look forward to eating them year after year. These foods can include a special roast turkey dinner, homemade bread, or Christmas cookies. Many times, foods have ethnic origins. Writer Linda Larsen recalls her grandmother's potato pancakes. "My paternal grandmother Clara made the most wonderful *lefse*. Lefse is a Norwegian potato pancake that we always served spread thinly with sweet butter and sprinkled with sugar. When properly made, it is melting, tender, nutty, and slightly sweet. Now my littlest sister is in charge of making lefse each Christmas from extra cooked potatoes made especially for this dish."[8]

Rituals are another part of treasured Christmas memories. Traveling to a tree farm to cut down the Christmas tree is a favorite activity repeated year after year by some families. Others enjoy driving around looking at holiday light displays. Decorating the Christmas tree is often the source of happy Christmas memories, and special ornaments take on great importance. Author Marcy Zitz writes, "One of my fondest memories of decorating the tree was putting on my favorite ornament, an ornament that has hung on every Christmas tree I have ever had."[9] These Christmas memories and traditions are what make the holiday special and cherished by so many people around the world.

Christmas has changed from a pagan holiday to a religious celebration to a time of togetherness and sharing. It has been transformed from a time of rowdiness and partying to a more family-centered celebration of generosity and kindness. No matter how people celebrate, Christmas traditions continue to delight and inspire people around the world.

Spread the Spirit

Christmas is a time to spread cheer and love. One way to do this is to volunteer to help others. There are many ways for young people to do this. Here are a few ideas:

1. Organize a holiday toy drive. Ask your school principal for permission to put up posters and collection boxes at school where students and their families can donate new or gently used toys. Gather up the toys and donate them to a local organization collecting for the needy.

2. Organize a "Warmth of Christmas" collection. Encourage friends, classmates, and family members to donate new gloves, mittens, hats, and scarves. Collect them and donate to a local charity.

3. Perform a "Deed a Day." Make a paper chain with twenty four links (one for every day of December before Christmas). On each link, write a good deed you can perform. Deeds can include shoveling a neighbor's walk or helping him or her with grocery shopping, helping a younger child

make a gift, reading to a younger child, helping a classmate with homework, or using your allowance to buy toys or canned goods for a local charity drive. Each day, read a link and perform the good deed.

4. Ask your family about volunteering at a local food kitchen or charity center. You might be able to wrap and/or distribute gifts or serve food to the needy.

5. Get a group of friends and family together and sing Christmas carols at a local hospital or nursing home.

GLOSSARY

agriculture—The science of cultivating soil, producing crops, and raising livestock.

ancient—Very old; relating to a remote period or to a time in early history.

census—A count of all the people in an area or a country.

charity—Money or other help given to people in need.

commercial—Having to do with buying and selling things.

controversial—Opposing viewpoints that sometimes cause an argument.

federal—Having to do with the central government.

festive—Cheerful.

folklore—Traditional customs, stories, and dances preserved among a people.

fortunate—Receiving some unexpected good.

immigrants—People who come from a country to live permanently in another country.

lavish—Fancy or overgenerous.

Middle Ages—European history between 500 and 1500 A.D.

Nativity—Jesus' birth; also, a display or scene to commemorate his birth.

pagan—A person who worships many gods.

pageants—A public show where people parade or act out historical scenes.

peasants—Poor people who work on farms, especially in Europe during the Middle Ages.

procession—A parade during a public festival or religious service.

Puritans—A group of Protestants in the 16th and 17th centuries who had strict religious beliefs and advocated simple ceremonies.

reformer—Someone who tries to change things.

revelry—Partying; celebration.

solemn—Serious; awe-inspiring.

tradition—Handing down customs and beliefs from one generation to the next.

CHAPTER NOTES

◆ Chapter 1. A Child Is Born

1. Luke 2: 6–7. May, Herbert G. and Bruce M. Metzer, eds. *The New Oxford Annotated Bible with the Apocrypha*, revised standard version (New York: Oxford University Press, 1977).

2. Luke 2: 8–11. *The New Oxford Annotated Bible with the Apocrypha*, revised standard version.

3. "Chronology of Jesus," *Wikipedia*, June 11, 2006, <http://en.wikipedia.org/wiki/Chronology_of_Jesus'_birth_and_death> (June 13, 2006).

4. Matthew 2: 2. *The New Oxford Annotated Bible with the Apocrypha*, revised standard version.

5. Matthew 2: 9. *The New Oxford Annotated Bible with the Apocrypha*, revised standard version.

6. "Chronology of Jesus," *Wikipedia*, June 11, 2006, <http://en.wikipedia.org/wiki/Chronology_of_Jesus'_birth_and_death> (June 13, 2006).

7. "The Birth of Jesus Christ," *2think.org*, 1997, <http://www.2think.org/hundredsheep/bible/birth.shtml> (June 13, 2006).

◆ Chapter 2. The History of Christmas

1. Stephen Nissenbaum, *The Battle for Christmas* (New York: Alfred A Knopf, 1996), p. 5.

2. Ace Collins, *Stories Behind the Great Traditions of Christmas* (Grand Rapids, Mich.: Zondervan, 2003), p. 11.
3. Ibid., p. 189.
4. "The History of Christmas," *The History Channel*, n.d., <http://www.historychannel.com/exhibits/holidays/christmas/real.html> (March 2, 2006).
5. Ibid.
6. Collins, p. 12.
7. Ibid., p. 13.
8. Collins, pp. 13–14.
9. "The History of Christmas," *The History Channel*.
10. Nissenbaum, p. 8.
11. "The History of Christmas," *The History Channel*.
12. Nissenbaum, p. 9.
13. Richard Howland Maxwell, "Pilgrim and Puritan: A Delicate Distinction," *Pilgrim Hall Museum*, March 2003, <http://www.pilgrimhall.org/PS NoteNewPilgrimPuritan.htm> (June 13, 2006).
14. Collins, pp. 14–15.
15. Richard Howland Maxwell, "Pilgrim and Puritan: A Delicate Distinction."
16. William Bradford, *Of Plymouth Plantation, 1620–1647* (New York: Alfred A. Knopf, 1952), p. 97.
17. "The History of Christmas," *The History Channel*.
18. Ibid.
19. Collins, p. 17.
20. "The History of Christmas," *The History Channel*.
21. George Washington Curtis, "Christmas," *Harper's New Monthly Magazine*, December 1883, p. 3.
22. "The History of Christmas," *The History Channel*.

23. Collins, pp. 95-96.
24. "Evolution of Santa," *The History of Christmas, The History Channel*, n.d., <http://www.history channel.com/exhibits/holidays/christmas/santa .html> (March 2, 2006).
25. Collins, p. 101.
26. Elliot Wigginton et al., eds., *A Foxfire Christmas* (Chapel Hill: N.C.: University of North Carolina Press, 1996), p. 43.
27. Ibid., pp. 65–70.
28. Penne L. Restad, *Christmas in America: A History* (New York: Oxford University Press, 1995), p. 52.

◆ Chapter 3. The Cultural Significance of Christmas

1. Penne L. Restad, *Christmas in America: A History* (New York: Oxford University Press, 1995), p. 44.
2. Ace Collins, *Stories Behind the Great Traditions of Christmas* (Grand Rapids, Mich.: Zondervan, 2003), p. 21.
3. Dr. Caron B. Goode, "Christmas Giving," *WomenOf.com*, December 12, 2005, <http://www.womenof.com/Articles/fc_12_12_05.asp> (March 2, 2006).
4. Mary D. Lankford, *Christmas Around the World* (New York: William Morrow, 1995), p. 23.
5. Karal Ann Marling, *Merry Christmas! Celebrating America's Greatest Holiday* (Cambridge, Mass.: Harvard University Press, 2000), p. 28.
6. M. Vivian Hughes, "A London Child of the Seventies," excerpted in *A London Christmas*,

compiled by Marina Cantacuzino (Gloucester, England: Alan Sutton Publishing Ltd., 1989), pp. 1–3.

7. Collins, p. 101.

8. Dawn Gibeau, "Happiest Christmas Does Not Go To Highest Bidder—Statement of Center for the Study of Commercialism," *National Catholic Reporter*, December 3, 1993.

9. Ibid.

◆ Chapter 4. Who Celebrates Christmas?

1. Ace Collins, *Stories Behind the Great Traditions of Christmas* (Grand Rapids, Mich.: Zondervan, 2003), p. 164.

2. Ibid.

3. Penne L. Restad, *Christmas in America: A History* (New York: Oxford University Press, 1995), p. 50.

4. Collins, p. 168.

5. Restad, p. 71.

6. George S. Hillard, ed. *Life, Letters, and Journals of George Ticknor*, 6th ed. (Boston: James R. Osgood, 1877), vol. 1, pp. 460–461.

7. "World Traditions," *The History of Christmas, The History Channel*, n.d., <http://www.history channel.com/exhibits/holidays/christmas/world .html> (March 2, 2006).

8. Mary D. Lankford, *Christmas Around the World* (New York: William Morrow, 1995), p. 28.

9. Ibid., p. 24.

10. "World Traditions," *The History of Christmas, The History Channel.*

11. Dr. Caron B. Goode, "Christmas Giving," *WomenOf.com*, December 12, 2005, <http://www.womenof.com/Articles/fc_12_12_05.asp> (March 2, 2006).

12. Marina Cantacuzino, compiler, *A London Christmas* (Gloucester, England: Alan Sutton Publishing Ltd., 1989), p. 38.

13. Restad, p. 176.

◆ Chapter 5. **Symbols of Christmas**

1. Penne L. Restad, *Christmas in America: A History* (New York: Oxford University Press, 1995), pp. 55–56.

2. Stephen Nissenbaum, *The Battle for Christmas* (New York: Alfred A Knopf, 1996), p. 73.

3. "Evolution of Santa," *The History of Christmas, The History Channel*, n.d., <http://www.history channel.com/exhibits/holidays/christmas/santa .html> (March 2, 2006).

4. "Christmas Trees," *The History of Christmas, The History Channel*, n.d., <http://www.history channel.com/exhibits/holidays/christmas/trees. html> (March 2, 2006).

5. Ibid.

6. Ibid.

7. Ace Collins, *Stories Behind the Great Traditions of Christmas* (Grand Rapids, Mich.: Zondervan, 2003), p. 152.

8. Ibid., pp. 154–155.

9. Ibid., pp. 157–158.

10. Ibid., p. 125.

11. Ibid., p. 128.

12. Dr. Caron B. Goode, "Christmas Giving," *WomenOf.com*, December 12, 2005, <http://www.womenof.com/Articles/fc_12_12_05.asp> (March 2, 2006).

13. Collins, pp. 139–140.

14. Ibid., pp. 141–142.

15. "Humbug! Christmas Steeped in Controversy," *FOX News.com*, December 20, 2004, <http://www.foxnews.com/printer_friendly_story/0,3566,141920,00.html> (March 3, 2006).

16. Ibid.

17. Cliff Walker, "Governments Should Not Erect Religious Displays," *Positive Atheism.org*, 2000, <http://www.positiveatheism.org/crt/holiday.htm> (June 13, 2006).

18. Ibid.

19. "Humbug! Christmas Steeped in Controversy," FOX News.com.

20. Ibid.

21. "The History of Christmas," *The History Channel*, n.d., <http://www.historychannel.com/exhibits/holidays/christmas/real.html> (March 2, 2006).

22. Collins, pp. 49–50.

23. "Evolution of Santa," The History of Christmas, *The History Channel*.

24. Karal Ann Marling, *Merry Christmas! Celebrating America's Greatest Holiday* (Cambridge, Mass.: Harvard University Press, 2000), p. 286.

25. Restad, p. 118.

26. Marling, p. 288.

27. Ibid., p. 289.
28. Ibid., p. 291.
29. Restad, p. 122.
30. Collins, p. 59.

◆ Chapter 6. Christmas Today

1. Penne L. Restad, *Christmas in America: A History* (New York: Oxford University Press, 1995), p. 104.
2. Dr. Caron B. Goode, "Christmas Giving," *WomenOf.com*, December 12, 2005, <http://www.womenof.com/Articles/fc_12_12_05.asp> (March 2, 2006).
3. Dawn Gibeau, "Happiest Christmas Does Not Go To Highest Bidder—Statement of Center for the Study of Commercialism," *National Catholic Reporter*, December 3, 1993
4. Bill McKibben, "Who Stole Christmas?" *Christian Century*, December 2, 1998,
5. Ibid.
6. Ibid.
7. Dr. Caron B. Goode, "Christmas Giving," *WomenOf.com*.
8. Linda Larsen, "Christmas Memories: Make Memories of Your Own," *About.com*, n.d., <http://busycooks.about.com/od/christmas/a/christmasmemori.htm> (June 13, 2006).
9. Marcy Zitz, "Christmas Memories: A Special Thanks to Moms and Dads," *About.com*, n.d., <http://familyinternet.about.com/library/blxmasmemory.htm> (June 13, 2006).

FURTHER READING

Books

Barth, Edna. *Holly, Reindeer, and Colored Lights: the Story of the Christmas Symbols.* New York: Clarion Books, 2000.

Bonnice, Sherry. *Christmas and Santa Claus Folklore.* Broomall, Penn.: Mason Crest Publishers, 2003.

Bowler, Gerry. *The World Encyclopedia of Christmas.* Toronto, Canada: McClelland and Stewart, 2000.

Kain, Karen. *The Nutcracker: Based on the Production by James Kudelka.* Toronto, Canada: Tundra Books, 2005.

Ross, Michael Elsohn. *Mexican Christmas.* Minneapolis, Minn.: Carolrhoda Books, 2002.

Vaughan, Jenny, and Penny Beauchamp. *Christmas Foods.* Chicago, Ill.: Heinemann Library, 2004.

INTERNET ADDRESSES

Christmas
<http://www.historychannel.com/exhibits/
holidays/christmas/index.html>
Learn more about Christmas from the History Channel.

"The Night Before Christmas"
<http://www.christmas-tree.com/stories/night
beforechristmas.html>
Read the famous Clement Clarke Moore poem at this site.

INDEX